MW01139188

The Living Desert

The Living Desert

Les Hiddins

PUFFIN BOOKS

Puffin Books
Penguin Books Australia Ltd
487 Maroondah Highway, PO Box 257
Ringwood, Victoria 3134, Australia
Penguin Books Ltd
Harmondsworth, Middlesex, England
Penguin Putnam Inc.
375 Hudson Street, New York, New York 10014, USA
Penguin Books Canada Limited
10 Alcorn Avenue, Toronto, Ontario, Canada, M4V 3B2
Penguin Books (N.Z.) Ltd
Cnr Rosedale and Airborne Roads, Albany, Auckland,
New Zealand
Penguin Books (South Africa) (Pty) Ltd
5 Watkins Street, Denver Ext 4, 2094, South Africa
Penguin Books India (P) Ltd
11, Community Centre, Panchsheel Park,
New Delhi 110 017, India

First published by Penguin Books Australia Ltd, 2000

10 9 8 7 6 5 4 3 2 1

Copyright © Les Hiddins, 2000
Copyright © This edition, form, concept and design
Penguin Books Australia Ltd, 2000

The moral right of the author has been asserted.

All rights reserved. Without limiting the rights under copyright
reserved above, no part of this publication may be reproduced,
stored in or introduced into a retrieval system, or transmitted,
in any form or by any means (electronic, mechanical,
photocopying, recording or otherwise), without the prior
written permission of both the copyright owner and the
above publisher of this book.

Printed in China by Midas Printing (Asia) Ltd

National Library of Australia
Cataloguing-in-Publication data

Hiddins, L. J., 1946–.
The living desert.

Includes index.
ISBN 0 14 130995 4.

1. Desert biology – Australia – Juvenile literature. 2.
Wilderness survival – Australia – Juvenile literature. 3.
Desert plants – Australia – Juvenile literature. 4. Desert
animals – Australia – Juvenile literature. I. Title.
(Series: discover wild Australia with the bush tucker man).

577.54

www.puffin.com.au

THE LIVING DESERT

Project Editor and Manager
Margaret Barca

Managing Editor
Astrid Browne

Design
Tony Palmer, Penguin Design Studio
and Sandy Coventry, P. A.G.E. Pty Ltd

Special thanks to
Carol Hiddins; Ray Pask (Geography Consultant);
Steve Strike (Outback Photographics); Bruce Rankin
(map illustration); Kay Ronai (Editor); Fay Donlevy
(Indexer); National Library of Australia, for permission
to reproduce historic images.

PHOTO CREDITS
All photos were taken by Steve Strike, Outback
Photographics unless otherwise stated below.

Abbreviations

AG	Andrew Gregory
JM	John Meier
LH	Les Hiddins
NF/RB	Nature Focus (Roger Brown)
NF/H&JB	Nature Focus (H & J Beste)
NLA	National Library of Australia
SP/RG	Stock Photos (Ross Green)
WA/NB	Wildflight Australia (Nicholas Birks)

Abbreviations for positions
t – top; b – bottom; l – left; r – right; c – centre;
fp – full page

Cover WA/NB (r). Back cover JM (fp).
Pages vii JM. 2 LH. 3 AG (r). 4–5 JM. 6 AG (b),
NF/ H&JB (r). 7 WA/NB (fp). 9 WA/NB (t). 12 LH (r).
16 LH (r). 17 LH (c). 18 LH (c). 21 LH (c). 25 WA/NB (c),
NF/RB (l). 31 NF/H&JB (b). 32 LH (t), WA/NB (b).
33 LH (b), SP/RG (r). 35 WA/NB (b). 36 LH (l), NLA (r).
37 NLA (l), NLA/S4579 (b), Telstra (r).

PUBLISHER'S NOTE
The author and publisher cannot take responsibility
for any illness, injury or ailment brought on through
consuming or handling plants.

This book is dedicated to all those young people who are keen to discover more about wild Australia.

Warning
Some bush foods are poisonous. Never handle or eat any bush tucker without checking with an adult if it's safe to do so.

Words printed in **bold** are explained in the Glossary on page 39.

Contents

Heart of Australia

Australia is the second driest continent in the world. More than two-thirds of the country is desert – **arid** or **semi-arid** land. It doesn't look like there's much life in those deserts, and you'd probably wonder how anything could survive. In fact, many animals and plants call this home. Some of them have adapted over time to live in this very harsh environment. And there are a few species you'd never think could survive, tucked away in the heart of Australia – like frogs, for example. Aboriginal people have also lived in some of these areas for thousands of years. They've adapted in their own way, learning to understand and live with the land.

Bearded dragon

GREAT SAN
DESERT

GIBSO
DESI

The Pinnacles

• Perth

The Simpson Desert

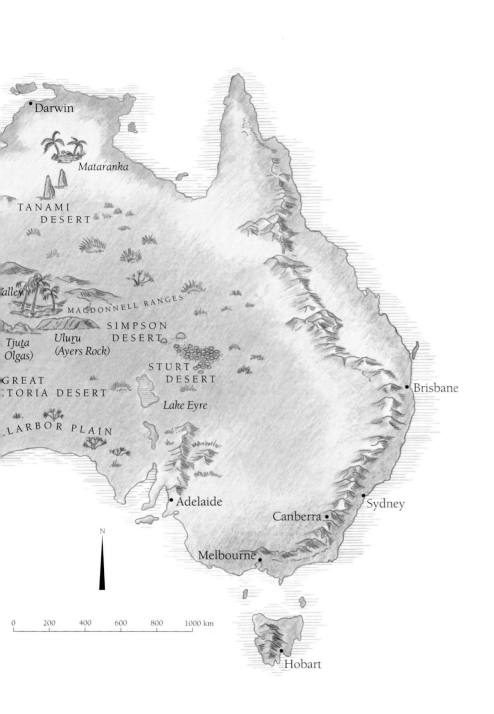

WHAT IS A DESERT?

A desert is an area that receives very low rainfall. In an arid area there is hardly any **vegetation** or animal life. A semi-arid area can support a little more plant and animal life.

In Australia's desert country, rainfall is very erratic and very unreliable. No one knows when it will rain next. Some years you might get a reasonable amount of rain, and then for several years no rain, or almost no rain. When it *does* rain, the water evaporates very quickly because of the heat.

Really, the whole of inland Australia is one type of desert or another. You can see the names of our major deserts on this map.

Map labels

- Darwin
- *Mataranka*
- TANAMI DESERT
- ...alley
- MACDONNELL RANGES
- SIMPSON DESERT
- *Uluru* (Ayers Rock)
- *Tju̱ta* Olgas)
- STURT DESERT
- GREAT ...CTORIA DESERT
- *Lake Eyre*
- ...LARBOR PLAIN
- Brisbane
- Adelaide
- Canberra
- Sydney
- Melbourne
- Hobart

N

0   200   400   600   800   1000 km

1

The Desert Country

Most people think of deserts as just being sand. That's not the case at all. In Australia, however, we do have some sandy deserts. The sand is often a yellowish-grey colour, but it usually has native plants that help stop the sand drifting away. Some of the sandy country is quite a strong red colour. That colour is caused by the high iron content in the sand. It looks as if the sand is almost rusty. In parts of the sandy country where there is very little plant life, the wind blows the sand into shapes and patterns, creating sand dunes, a bit like waves in the ocean. We also have rocky and stony deserts, and mountain deserts.

HOW HOT?

Deserts have extreme temperatures. It really heats up in the daytime. In the summer, the average temperature might be 37–39° C. It can reach 50° C or more in some parts. And that sun is scorching. Of course, at night there are no clouds to trap the heat. The temperature can drop quite rapidly and even get down to freezing point. At night in 'winter' it can be frosty.

DESERT OASIS

Australia wasn't always so dry. Millions of years ago, this continent was covered in **rainforest**. Hidden away in some of the ranges are sheltered pockets where there is still water and signs of the lush vegetation that was once here. Such places provide a **refuge** for rare plants, a place for animals and, sometimes, for people to shelter.

Palm Valley

Palm Valley, in the heart of the **Red Centre**, is a very special refuge. The sheltered valley is a real **oasis**, and home to around 3000 rare red cabbage palms. Those palms don't grow anywhere else in the world. The nearest related palms are 1000 km north, near Mataranka.

Spinifex desert
Large areas of **Outback** Australia
are covered by spinifex. Some
people call it porcupine grass
because it is prickly like a
porcupine. This grass can survive
tremendous heat and drought.
The roots grow very deep, and help
hold the sand together. Even after
a fire, when the top of the spinifex
is dead, the roots will still be there,
holding the sand together.

Gibber desert
'**Gibber**' comes from an Aboriginal
word meaning 'stone', and these
deserts are covered in millions of small
stones. You won't see much plant life
in a gibber desert, because the clay
beneath the stones is compact and
hard. Yet even in the gibber deserts,
some plants and animals survive.

3

Desert Landscape

Australia's arid country has some spectacular **landforms**. These landforms have been eroded and weathered over millions of years. When heavy rains come, floods wash away the soil and cut into the stone. Wind also flakes away soft rock and carves strange shapes. There are not many plants to hold the soil together. The few plants that are there push their roots down, searching for water, weakening the rock as they go. The extreme temperatures in the desert, from tremendous heat to freezing cold, can make the rock expand and then contract. That weakens it, too, and finally the rock might shatter or break away.

Although some of the desert **outcrops**, like Uluru, and mountains, like the MacDonnell Ranges in Central Australia, are impressive, they are all that remains of the giant mountains that once existed here. The Red Centre is one of the most ancient landscapes on earth.

The Pinnacles

In Western Australia, these strange limestone outcrops (*below*) were formed around the roots of plants 20 000 years ago. Over time, the shapes of the Pinnacles changed and were exposed as sand and soil blew away.

Kata Tjuta (The Olgas)

Kata Tjuta is from an Aboriginal word meaning 'many-headed', and the huge rocks look like a jumble of domes. There are valleys and **gorges** between the domes. The highest point, Mt Olga, is 546 metres above the ground.

Uluru (Ayers Rock)

Uluru (*above*), in the Red Centre, is a huge **monolith**, rising up out of the sand plain. It's about 300 metres high, and the walk around the base is 9 km. Moisture, oxygen in the air, and heavy rains are still slowly wearing away the red rock.

Mt Conner

Not far from Uluru is Mt Conner, a flat-topped mountain or **mesa**. It's a very ancient landform – probably about 150 million years older than either Uluru or Kata Tjuta.

Waiting for Rain

When rain comes, the desert takes on a whole new look. Rivers may flood. Trees and shrubs that have been **dormant** for many seasons come to life. Wildflowers bloom. Seeds suddenly **germinate**, sprout, flower and produce seeds. They rush through their life cycle in weeks, before the water has gone. With the rains, insects emerge from their eggs and cocoons. These insects help **pollinate** flowers, carrying the nectar from one flower to another. Insects also hurry through their life cycle, feeding and mating and producing young.

Water-holding frogs

These frogs are able to store extra water in their bodies. They burrow down a metre or so, and wait for heavy rains. They might have to wait two years – maybe more. Meanwhile their dead skin forms a thin casing, like a loose bag, to help them stay moist. When heavy rain comes, the frogs eat through the skin and come out of hiding. They quickly mate, lay and fertilise eggs. Those eggs have to hatch and develop into tadpoles, and then frogs, before the water dries up again. It's a real race against time.

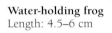

Water-holding frog
Length: 4.5–6 cm

Empty rivers

There are rivers in the arid Outback, but a lot of the time they're empty. All you see is a wide, dry riverbed, sometimes with trees growing in the middle of it. But you'd be wise never to camp in a riverbed, because all of a sudden, if it does rain, the river can fill and flood. The Finke River (*above*), in Central Australia, is one of the oldest rivers in the world. Parts of it are about 350 million years old.

When the rain comes, flowers bloom, even in sandy country.

Centralian tree frog
Length: 4 cm

Frogs in the desert
Some frogs in the desert stay close
to permanent waterholes or dams.
Burrowing frogs dig down through the
mud and wait for the next wet period
to come.

The tiny, smooth-skinned centralian
tree frog (*above*) lives in arid country,
but stays close to permanent waterholes.
In hot weather these frogs huddle together
under a stone or rocks to stay cool.

Shield shrimp
Hidden in muddy rockpools and
waterholes in desert areas are tiny
crustaceans known as shield shrimp.
Their fertilised eggs can survive soaring
temperatures and freezing cold as well as
drought. When there is no water, the eggs
lie in the dried mud, or are blown about,
until the next rains. Within days of rain
millions of shrimp fill small rockpools
and puddles. As the water dries up, the
shrimp die, but those that have mated
leave fertilised eggs. These eggs will
survive until the next heavy rains.

Shield shrimp
Length: 3 cm

7

Water for Survival

In the desert, water can be the difference between life and death. It's essential for survival. Plants, animals and people all have special ways to conserve water, to find water or to make water last. Some of these ways are quite surprising.

Thorny devil
Length: 15 cm

Water in the ranges

Much of the desert country in Australia is flat but there are rocky outcrops and hills and ranges. These higher parts tend to get rainfall more often than other areas. Aboriginal people knew that water could often be found in crevices and hollows in these places – sometimes long after it had rained. Animals would also come to these places looking for water.

Water catcher

The spikes on the thorny devil aren't just for looks. They help collect drops of moisture and dew, which then run along tiny channels to the corner of its mouth, so this lizard can drink while it is on the run.

Zebra finch

Zebra finches are found all over arid and semi-arid country. They usually move in flocks, sometimes huge flocks of a thousand or more birds as they swoop in for water. They get very thirsty because they are seed-eaters, so they need to drink often. If you see zebra finches, you can be pretty sure there's water close by.

Zebra finch
Length: 9 cm

Hidden water

Water collects in the hollows of certain trees, like gum trees. You can also get water from the root systems of some trees, like the desert oak (*above*) and the batwing coral tree. You dig down to get the roots, then break or cut them into lengths and drain the water.

Upside-down rivers

Some of the rivers and creeks in the arid country, especially in the Red Centre, are almost like upside-down waterways. Most of the time, there's no water in them. But don't be fooled. If you dig into that riverbed, you'll find water in many places. That's knowledge Aboriginal people traditionally used when they were moving around the country during dry times.

Frog in the throat

Aboriginal people knew that water-holding frogs burrowed down under certain trees, like the batwing coral tree, waiting for heavy rain. During a drought or a very dry spell, some tribes might dig down looking for those frogs, to get the water from them. That's a hard way to get a drink, but it's also a reminder of just how precious water is in the desert.

Signs of water

Sometimes out in the desert you might come across rock carvings that show circles (*above*). The circles imitate the effect you get when you throw a rock into water. Those circles were carved by Aboriginal people to let others know that there was water in the area.

Desert Plants

Over time, plants that live in the desert have adapted to very dry conditions in different ways. Some grasses and flowering plants, which only last one season, have seeds with a tough coating. The seeds can lie on top of the soil waiting until there is enough water for them to germinate. Sometimes that might take years. When the rains come, the plants spring to life. The seeds shoot, and in no time at all flowers have bloomed – and died – leaving new seeds.

STOP!
Some desert plants simply stop growing if there is a drought. Others drop their leaves to reduce the amount of water needed. Some plants have shallow roots near the surface to catch rain, but they also have roots that reach way, way down to get water. Some plants look dead, but within just a few hours of rain they sprout fresh new leaves.

Catching the rain
Like many desert trees and shrubs, the hardy mulga tree has narrow leaves that tend to point upwards. When it rains, the water is channelled along the leaves, then drips down the trunk to soak the ground around the roots.

Paper daisies cover the ground after heavy rain in the Red Centre.

Sturt's desert pea

The seeds of Sturt's desert pea only germinate when there has been enough rainfall for the flower to complete its life cycle. It needs a really heavy rainfall to start those seeds sprouting.

Sturt's desert rose

Sturt's desert rose only produces its soft, large pink flowers after heavy rains. If there is no water available, the plant dies off, but its seeds can survive for up to ten years.

Putting down roots

The tap roots – they're the main roots – of the desert oak reach way down, sometimes tens of metres, in search of water. The tree grows very slowly until those roots can get enough water for the tree to survive and grow to full size. The leaves are really just tiny scales, so they do not lose moisture easily.

Spiky spinifex

Spinifex thrives in arid country, growing in tough clumps in deep sand or rocky ground. The long, strap-like leaves are flat at first. After the first dry season, however, the blades fold over so that they don't lose unnecessary moisture. They curl in and become quite spiky.

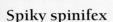

Parakeelya purple

After rain, you'll sometimes see flowers such as the bright purple parakeelya (*right*). This plant soaks up as much moisture as possible from the soil and stores it in the leaves. The leaves become quite plump. The flowers usually only open for a single day. The plant quickly produces seeds and then dies off.

Survival Skills

Long ago, Aboriginal people mastered the art of survival in the desert. One of their great skills was the ability to observe and understand the country around them. They would look *into* the countryside. They'd think about what could help them survive. The colour of a leaf, the arrival of a certain bird, or tracks on the ground might all be important clues to what food could be found. That could be pretty important if your next meal depended on it.

HUNTING AND GATHERING

Like Aboriginal people all over Australia, desert Aborigines were nomadic, moving from place to place, hunting and gathering their food. In the harsh desert **environment**, however, survival was especially hard. Temperatures are extreme, and plants, animals and water are all scarce. Many tribes were constantly moving across very large areas of country to find enough food and water.

WOMEN'S WORK

The women were responsible for gathering seeds, nuts, fruit and small animals, as well as digging for **yams**. They had – many of them *still* have – a tremendous ability to remember where they saw a particular bush, when it might have fruit or be flowering, or where they last saw some signs of underground bulbs or **tubers** that might be ready to eat.

Out all day

A very large part of the day was spent chasing up bush tucker. Some bush foods are only in season part of the time. Some bushes might only have a few ripe berries or figs. And you had to get there early – a bit of wind, some insects, a few birds and there'd be nothing left.

Digging for yams
Aboriginal women could recognise a crack in the ground, and follow it to a certain spot before digging to reveal a yam, which is like a potato.

What's to eat?

The men hunted kangaroos, wallabies, emus and so on, but the women provided the bulk of the day-to-day food. They dug for yams, caught small lizards and goannas and looked for edible grubs and insects. As they went about gathering food, they might chew on the sweet gum from certain trees, or suck the nectar from edible flowers such as the honey grevillea.

Honey grevillea

BUSH MEDICINE

As well as using plants for food, Aboriginal people used them to make medicine. They needed to treat wounds and sores, cuts, burns from fires, toothache and other common complaints. For example, they would grind the seeds of the desert quandong (*below*) then mix the powder with water and put it on skin sores. They used the bark from the conkerberry tree to make a medicinal liquid for sore eyes. They chewed certain leaves to relieve toothache.

Desert quandongs

Water in the desert

Aboriginal people living in the desert seem to have an instinct for where to find water. They know how to get water from tree roots and from plants. They know where to dig into dry riverbeds and how to find water hidden near rocky outcrops.

13

Making Tracks

Many Australian animals are **nocturnal** – they are out and about at night. In the desert, the only sign of some creatures might be their tracks on the sand – and even those tracks might be blown away during the day. The intense heat means that some other animals only come out when they need to drink, usually in the cool of the morning or late in the day. They too might leave tracks, often near a waterhole. For Aboriginal people, tracking animals was part of the daily search for bush tucker. They were experts at it.

LOOKING FOR TRACKS

One of the best places to look for tracks is near a waterhole, where the tracks stay in the soil as it dries. Have a close look at the sand, too, especially early in the morning. Around the clumps of spinifex is another good place to search. Quite a few creatures make their home in that spinifex – native mice, lizards and geckoes. If they hear or see something, they quickly scurry into the spiky clumps of grass.

Hopping along

The paired tracks of a hopping marsupial near the plains might mean a red kangaroo. Closer to rocky outcrops, the tracks could be those of a euro. The euros, or hill kangaroos, stay pretty close to shady outcrops. You might see the zig-zagging trail of a little spinifex hopping-mouse *(right)* or the long claws of an emu. The size and the depth of the imprint give you a clue to the size of the animals.

Lizard feet

These close footprints belong to the thorny devil, a type of lizard. That's the thorny devil on the opposite page, scooting along on the sand.

Follow that lizard!

These tracks show the claws of a perentie, a giant lizard. You can see where the tail drags along the sand.

Sliding along

A curving track might be made as a small legless lizard or snake moves along. A blind snake (a smooth, worm-like snake that spends most of its time underground) has slithered along this sand.

When the tracks lead to a particular type of burrow or hole, that's another clue to the type of animal.

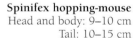

Spinifex hopping-mouse
Head and body: 9–10 cm
Tail: 10–15 cm

Hopping-mouse

Look for the tracks of the spinifex hopping-mouse between clumps of spinifex.

15

Desert Bush Foods

There is food in the desert – *if* you know what to look for. In order to survive, desert Aborigines needed to use *all* the resources they could. Traditionally, they used a very wide range of plants and animals. Some of these foods were a regular part of the diet. Others would only be eaten occasionally, as a special treat, or when they were in season for a short time.

Witchetty grubs

The plump white **larva** of a cossid moth, known as a witchetty grub, can often be found in the roots of the witchetty bush. Aboriginal women would dig for these grubs. The women and children would probably eat some of the grubs raw, and maybe take the rest back to camp to cook on hot coals. These tasty morsels provided protein and fats – important in the desert diet. Witchetty grubs are still quite popular as a bush 'snack'.

Mulga tree gum

The sticky, waxy, red growth on the branches of the mulga tree is made by a lerp scale insect. The gum, like honey, could be sucked off the branches. Children, in particular, liked to chew the gum because it was sweet.

Lerp scale

When a lerp scale insect sucks the sap of eucalyptus leaves it creates a white, crusty powder, or lerp. Aboriginal people might scrape the powder off and eat it. It has a pleasant, sugary, eucalyptus taste. Or they might soak the lerp in water to make a drink.

Bush apples

Hanging from various eucalypt trees in parts of the desert country are round, woody growths known as bush apples or bush coconuts. Inside there's a pink or white lining, with an edible insect grub. That grub looks like a yellow sac of moisture. Aboriginal people would eat the grub and the lining raw.

Bush apple
Grub length: 4 cm

Live honey pots

Honey ants, or honey pot ants, can only be found in a very tiny area in the desert country in Central Australia. The worker honey ants gather nectar and honeydew, then feed it to other ants. These ants store the honey in their bodies and become bloated to about the size of a grape. Then they hang in the nest until the queen or other worker ants need the honey during a drought.

Honey ant
Length: about 2–2.5 cm when filled with nectar

Desert yams

After rainfall the green, heart-shaped leaves of the desert yam often appear in sandy soil, scrambling around old trees and bushes. Starchy **tubers**, a bit like sweet potatoes, grow about half a metre underground. Aboriginal people would usually roast the tubers, which are quite juicy and tasty – that's if the tubers are not too old.

Prized bush tucker

Honey ants were – and still are – a special treat. Aboriginal women from the Papunya area would find the nest, then dig down for a metre or more for a handful of the sweet ants. They don't swallow the ants, but suck the honey from the swollen abdomens.

Bush Fruits

The fruits you find in the desert country often have names like European fruits – wild oranges and wild berries – but they don't look or taste much like the fruits we know. They're not big and juicy. They're not always sweet. They were still pretty popular as bush tucker though. Sometimes desert tribes might eat the leaves, the young roots or the sweet nectar from the flowers.

Native rock figs have a dry, slightly sweetish taste. Dried figs were sometimes collected and ground into a paste to eat.

BUSH BANANAS

Bush bananas grow in the **arid zone,** sometimes along creek beds and watercourses. In order to reach the scarce water supply, the roots reach down into the ground far below the surface.

The small green fruit has tiny green seeds, which are attached to fine white threads. These green seeds are edible. When the fruit matures, the seeds turn black, the fruit bursts open, and the threads blow away, spreading the seeds.

Hot bananas

The flowers of the bush banana are a creamy-green colour and sweet in flavour. Aboriginal people would eat these flowers and sometimes even the young leaves. They would eat the young fruit raw, but when it was more mature they might cook it over hot coals.

Native rock figs

You'll see native rock figs in desert areas, often near a creek bed. The figs are about the size of a marble. The trees look a bit stunted. In arid areas, the roots of these trees trail down into rock crevices in search of water. If you followed those roots, you'd often come across the source of water.

WILD ORANGES

There are a number of different plants called 'wild oranges', which grow in parts of the desert country. This one goes by the scientific or Latin name of *Capparis mitchellii*. The 'mitchellii' part tells us it was named after the famous Australian explorer Sir Thomas Mitchell.

Night flowering

The wild orange tree is small – around 4 metres tall – and the leaves are a dull green.

The creamy-yellow coloured flowers have delicate long stamens. Like some other desert plants, the flowers open at night, but they wither by the end of the next day.

The fruit is about the size of a small lemon. The sweet, orange-coloured pulp tastes a bit like mango. The seeds of the fruit stick to the pulp. The branches on the young trees are thorny and sharp. They were traditionally used to help catch bats, which were flushed out of bush caves.

Bush Cooking

Aboriginal people in the desert ate many foods raw. However, some foods needed preparation. Meat was an important part of the diet, and that might be a kangaroo, or lizard, an emu or a bush turkey – whatever the hunters could kill. The meat would be cooked on hot coals, or baked in hot ashes. Fruits that had dried out might be soaked in water to soften them up. Seeds were also important. For one thing, they were a very reliable source of nutrition.

Going to seed
Some seeds were roasted, then ground into a paste. That paste might be eaten raw, or cooked into damper, a type of bread. Other seeds were soaked and mashed up with water to make a drink. Some were poisonous and needed special treatment before they could be eaten.

Honey flowers
Hakea or corkwood trees have flowers with a sweet, honey-like nectar. Aboriginal people would suck the nectar from the flowers. Sometimes they might dunk the flowers in water to make a sweet drink.

The seed pods of hakea trees split open and blow away, spreading the seed. Aborigines ate the seeds from certain hakea trees.

Hakea pod
Length: 2–5 cm

Grinding stones
In the desert country, the seeds from grasses, trees, shrubs and herbs were all used. In most cases, the seeds would be ground to make a type of flour or paste. Grinding stones, like this one, are sometimes still found near traditional Aboriginal camping sites, particularly if there is a good source of water nearby.

What's cooking?
Food was usually cooked on hot coals or buried in hot ashes. Lizards and snakes were usually cooked whole.

Acacia seeds
There are plenty of mulga trees in the arid and semi-arid areas of Australia. The seed pods of certain mulga trees would be collected when the pods were still green. They might be eaten raw or cooked over hot earth. The dried seeds might be collected in a wooden dish, then ground up, using traditional stones, before being eaten.

21

Birds of a Feather

In the desert you find many birds that move in large flocks. You might see – and hear – hundreds or even thousands of budgerigars, or galahs, flying along or swooping on a waterhole. Birds seem to cope quite well with life in the desert. Their feathers provide a type of **insulation** from the hot days and cold nights. In the desert, birds are most likely to be seen early in the day, or after the sun has gone down.

Galah
Length: 35 cm

Those sharp beaks are perfect for cracking open seeds.

WHAT A GALAH!

You tend to see galahs in groups, from around 30 to as many as a thousand. The noise they make is fantastic – an ear-piercing screech, especially if there's a gang of them. When they fly, they flap along, moving erratically from side to side. Maybe that's why we say someone is a silly galah . . .

Galahs are not that silly though. They adjust their breeding depending on the seasons. If there has been good rain, they might lay five or more eggs. During a drought they may only lay one egg, or none at all. I reckon that's pretty clever.

BIG BIRD

A full-grown emu, at around 2 metres tall, is a very big bird. In fact, it's the second biggest of the world's flightless birds. Emus survive pretty well in arid country, staying mainly in pairs, or small groups. You don't see them so much in Central Australia, but quite a few of them roam around the dry country in the south-west of Queensland.

Emu eggs

Emus lay around six to 11 eggs. It's the male emu that sits on the eggs and then looks after the young chicks. Those eggs are very big and they change from a dull green in the first few days to a shiny black colour. Emu eggs were a favourite bush tucker. Emu meat was also considered a delicacy. Emus can run quite fast – up to 48 km an hour – so hunting them was serious work.

Emu egg
Length: about 13.5 cm

Emu
Height: 2 metres

Spinifex pigeon
Length: 20 cm

SPINIFEX PIGEONS

One bird that you'll definitely come across in the desert is the spinifex pigeon. They stay in small flocks – maybe 15 or so birds – and they're quite at home in the hot arid country. They eat mainly dry grasses and seeds, which means they need to drink often, so they tend to stay near water. If you see a flock of these birds, you'll know that there is water not too far away.

What's that whistling?

When the spinifex pigeons flap their wings, they make a metallic whistling sound. It's fairly distinctive. They usually fly quite fast and low. You might also see them dodging around the spinifex and over rocks, searching for seeds.

23

Where Eagles Fly

You can find the wedge-tailed eagle in most parts of Australia, but they are a real symbol of the Outback. They are very much at home in arid country. A majestic wedge-tailed eagle, or 'wedgie', hovering high above the land, is quite a sight. Majestic to us, maybe, but frightening for some creatures, because the eagle is a powerful hunter – a raptor, or bird of prey. They have extraordinary vision and powerful talons.

Soaring high
Eagles soar at between 200 and 1000 metres above the ground – high enough to escape some of the desert's heat. As they fly, a stream of air across the feathers helps cool the body. Their wingspan can be over 2 metres – perfect for catching the thermal currents, the gusts of air that help carry them along.

Eagles don't need to drink very often, as they get most of the moisture they need from the food they eat.

Eagle eyes
Like all birds of prey, eagles have amazingly good eyesight. They can see the slightest movement hundreds of metres away. Experts believe an eagle's vision is three times sharper than that of a human. Eagles can spot prey up to 1.5 km away.

Nesting instincts
Eagles build their nests high in trees or rocky outcrops. Some years they build a new nest. Other times they 'renovate' the existing nest, carrying in fresh sticks and leaves to line it. The end result can look pretty messy. A nest that has been used for some years might end up weighing 100 kg or more.

White to black

Eagle chicks are covered in soft, white downy feathers. The young wedgies are a brownish colour with reddish-brown heads and wings. As they get older their feathers become black. The feathers extend down the legs, right to the toes.

Hunt to kill

Once they see their prey, eagles can dive at over 80 km an hour, swooping on their victim. Rabbits, birds and reptiles such as lizards are their main prey. They hit the animal with their claws open, then apply a fierce grip as they carry their food back to the nest.

Flying solo

Eagles often fly and hunt alone. They will, however, gather in a group to feed on a carcass, a dead animal left by hunters, or a 'road-kill', an animal knocked down by a vehicle.

Eagle
Length: 1–1.2 metres
Wingspan: to 2.5 metres

Desert Creatures

Life is tough in the desert for animals as well as people. The fight for survival includes coping with the fierce heat and scorching sun, lack of water, and the need to avoid, escape from, or sometimes just to trick the enemy.

Desert camouflage

Many desert creatures are **camouflaged** by their colour. Others are strangely patterned so that it's hard to distinguish them from their surroundings. They seem to disappear into the landscape, concealed by rocks and shadows. Many of them are sandy yellow or reddish-brown, and some (especially lizards) change colour depending on the colours around them.

This little gecko almost fades into the reddish rock background.

Armed for protection

And if camouflage isn't enough, some creatures have armed themselves. The spiny-tailed monitor (*above*) has rows of spiny scales – dangerous if it lashes out with its tail. The thorny devil, a type of lizard, looks frightening with its strange spikes but it's really quite harmless.

Spiny-tailed monitor
Head and body: to 23.5 cm
Total length: to 78 cm

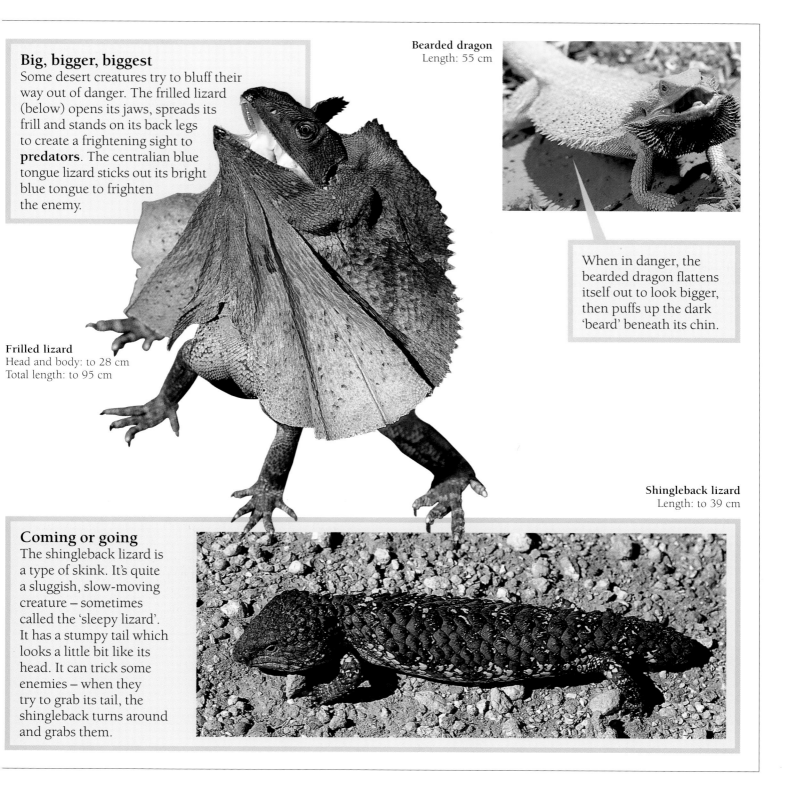

Big, bigger, biggest

Some desert creatures try to bluff their way out of danger. The frilled lizard (below) opens its jaws, spreads its frill and stands on its back legs to create a frightening sight to **predators**. The centralian blue tongue lizard sticks out its bright blue tongue to frighten the enemy.

Bearded dragon
Length: 55 cm

When in danger, the bearded dragon flattens itself out to look bigger, then puffs up the dark 'beard' beneath its chin.

Frilled lizard
Head and body: to 28 cm
Total length: to 95 cm

Shingleback lizard
Length: to 39 cm

Coming or going

The shingleback lizard is a type of skink. It's quite a sluggish, slow-moving creature – sometimes called the 'sleepy lizard'. It has a stumpy tail which looks a little bit like its head. It can trick some enemies – when they try to grab its tail, the shingleback turns around and grabs them.

Lizards and Snakes

Reptiles, like lizards and snakes, are probably more at home in the desert than any other animal. Lizards in particular have developed some clever ways of dealing with the desert conditions. You don't see them that often, though. Some of them only come out at night; many are quite small; others are very well camouflaged; some are fast and hide at the slightest sound. Lizards have quite a few enemies – eagles, snakes, dingoes, and even other lizards. Many lizards, and snakes, were also considered good bush tucker by desert tribes.

Wipe those eyes

This little knob-tail gecko, like most geckoes, hunts at night for spiders and ants. Those enormous eyes help a gecko see in the dark. Geckoes can't blink, but their eyes are covered with a transparent or clear lid. They frequently lick the lids with their tongue to keep the eyes clean.

Knob-tail gecko
Length: to 13 cm

TYPES OF LIZARDS

In Australia, we have five types or families of lizard. There are monitors (some people call them goannas), dragons, skinks, geckoes and legless lizards.

In the heat of the day

Lizards are cold-blooded – that means they can't keep their bodies at a regular temperature like we do. They need to move in and out of the sun and shade. Many lizards – especially goannas, dragons and skinks – are out and about during the day.

Central netted dragon
Length: to 28 cm

Central netted dragon

The central netted dragon will sometimes stand with its legs stretched up to avoid the heat of the ground. To escape the extreme desert temperatures, it will burrow underground and cover the entrance to the burrow with dirt.

SLEEPY SNAKES

Snakes are perfectly adjusted to the desert. They are cold-blooded like lizards. Their body temperature changes according to the temperature around them.

The carpet python usually curls up and sleeps in the day, then feeds at night. Their reddish-brown colouring is quite an effective camouflage. These pythons eat small mammals and birds – they squeeze them until they cannot breathe, then eat them whole.

Carpet python
Length: 2–4 metres

Gould's sand monitor
Length: up to 1.6 metres

Gould's sand monitor

This sand monitor is quite widespread in Australia, but the dry country is a good place to see a big one: they can grow to 1.6 metres. They're powerful and they're very fast runners. Like other monitors and snakes they have a forked tongue. Monitors and dragons tend to run on their two back legs – quite a frightening sight, especially if they're headed your way. These sand monitors were a very popular bush tucker – in some areas they still are.

Perentie – the giant lizard

The perentie, Australia's biggest lizard, is a monitor lizard or goanna. Despite its size, its blotchy brown, black and creamy colouring can make it difficult to spot. The perentie is a tough hunter. It eats small **mammals**, large insects and reptiles, including other lizards. It swallows them whole, without chewing.

Perentie
Length: up to 2.5 metres

Mammals and Marsupials

Kangaroos and wallabies, **marsupial** mice, bandicoots, bats – you'll find them all in the desert country. Of course, they're not all found in all areas. You might find a big mob of red kangaroos in western Queensland, but in other areas you might only see a few. Quite a lot of Australia's mammals are nocturnal. Others are burrowers that hide underground from the scorching heat. All in all, it's not that easy to spot some of these unique animals.

MAMMAL OR MARSUPIAL?

Mammals are animals (including humans) who feed their young on milk. Marsupials are animals that raise their young in a pouch. Some native Australian animals, like kangaroos, are both mammals *and* marsupials.

Red kangaroo
Height: 2 metres

KANGAROO OR WALLABY?

Kangaroos and wallabies are really all the one family. Larger **species** are usually called kangaroos and smaller ones wallabies. The big red kangaroos spend more time out on the open plains. Smaller, stockier wallabies stay closer to rocky country and shade.

Big red

Red kangaroos are big – up to 2 metres tall. They're able to travel across large areas in search of food. They can move fast too, covering up to 60 km an hour. In one leap they can cover 9 metres. They mainly feed at night, or in the day if the weather is cooler, and eat native grasses or herbs. If that grass has enough moisture, they can get by without needing much to drink. In a drought, when food is short, they stop breeding.

Hill kangaroo

The euro is a stocky kangaroo, smaller than the red kangaroo, but also very at home in the hot, dry Outback. They stay close to hilly country, sheltering in rocky areas, before heading out at night for a feed. They're very hardy. They can eat poor quality grass and tough spinifex and last for months without drinking water.

Euro
Head and body: 55–110 cm
Tail: 53–90 cm

Spinifex hopping-mouse

The tiny spinifex hopping-mouse can also survive without drinking water. It gets enough moisture from the insects and seeds it eats. During the day the mice sleep in underground burrows, huddled in together so they don't lose moisture from their bodies. They appear at night, hopping and running on their long back legs, zig-zagging in and out of clumps of spinifex.

Spinifex hopping-mouse
Head and body: 9–10 cm. Tail: 10–15 cm

Mala
Head and body: 31–39 cm
Tail: 25–30 cm

Mala

The mala, or rufous hare-wallaby, is now quite rare. This tiny little wallaby lives among the spinifex, sheltering from the heat, darting out for a bit of food. When it's really hot, the mala digs a fairly deep burrow and goes underground.

31

Insects and Spiders

The desert country certainly has its share of insects and spiders. The insect population in particular can vary a great deal depending on the weather. A drought might wipe out large numbers. When the weather becomes wetter those insects could multiply rapidly. In the desert, spiders and insects tend to hide away, especially when the sun is out. They mainly hunt for food at night.

Where are they?

Many desert spiders are burrowing spiders, making their nests underground. The scorpion's spiral burrow might be up to a metre deep. Spiders might also stay under a stone, or under a bush. If they do come out, most of them move pretty fast to stay out of the heat. Many ants tunnel underground.

Itchy grubs' hairy home

Hairy processionary caterpillars, or itchy grubs as they're known, join up in a long line – or procession – when moving about. They usually only come out in the cool of the evening. During the day they shelter in their pale silky bag nest. If you ever see one of those nests, stay well away – the hairs on the caterpillars and in the nest cause a severe burning skin sensation. Very itchy, very nasty.

Wolf spider
Body length: 1.6 cm

The trapdoor lid of a wolf spider's burrow is very clever.

Mulga ant mounds

Mulga ants build impressive mound nests, often under a mulga tree. They create a little wall around the nest with sticks. No one's really too sure why. In the flat mulga country, however, sudden floods can leave a sheet of water across the ground and that mound may well help save the nest.

Caterpillar Dreaming

In the Red Centre, the Aboriginal tribe known as the Western Arrernte call the MacDonnell Ranges *Yeparanya* or 'hairy caterpillars'. They reckon the folds of the mountains look just like these grubs. According to the Dreamtime legend, the giant caterpillar spirit was responsible for creating these mountains, and that's how they got the name Yeparanya.

Warning colours

The gold-spotted black grasshopper, or monistria, doesn't hide. Its bright colours warn lizards and birds that it's poisonous and not to eat it.

Monistria grasshopper
Length: about 3 cm

Scorpion stinger

Scorpions shelter in their cool burrows during the day, and hunt insects at night. They grab their prey with their front pincers and then strike with the stinger in their tail. The female gives birth to live young, who immediately climb onto the mother's back. The baby scorpions remain there for about two weeks until they're old enough to hunt for themselves. Scorpions in Australia are not deadly, though they do bite.

Masters of disguise

Grasshoppers often blend in with the surroundings to protect themselves. This grasshopper looks like a leaf or stick. Others look like pebbles or grass.

Scorpion
Length: 10 cm

33

Feral Animals

The desert is a very harsh environment, but it's also very fragile and very carefully balanced. In some areas that balance has been changed. Towns and cattle stations have been set up. Animals that have been brought in from overseas and allowed to go wild, or feral, have also caused tremendous damage. They eat the native plants and kill native animals. Some of our unique animal species are now rare. For them, life in the desert is tougher than ever. We need to protect the desert and our native animals – they are a very special part of Australia.

Exploring camels

Camel were brought into Australia in the 1800s by the early explorers. They played an important role in the exploration of this country and were also used to transport goods. When railways and trucks were introduced, however, those camels were let free. Today, it's estimated there could be 100 000 feral camels roaming the Outback. They're competing with native animals for plant food.

Rabbits run wild

Since they were first introduced into Australia in the 1850s, rabbits have run wild in parts of the country. Rabbit plagues have destroyed the vegetation in whole areas. Rabbits compete with the native wildlife, eating the same food. The rabbits multiply in huge numbers. A rabbit might give birth to twenty or twenty-five rabbits in a year. Our native animals are slow breeders. Although the number of rabbits has been reduced it's still a problem.

Shipping camels

These days, the Australian camel is prized as breeding stock. Some wild camels are being caught and shipped to Saudi Arabia in the Middle East.

Foxes

Foxes are not native to Australia, but they cope well with the semi-arid environment. They are meat-eaters and kill small animals. They hide in burrows in the day and hunt at night, when many native mice and marsupials are about.

Horses and donkeys

Like camels, horses and donkeys were brought into the Outback to help transport goods. Explorers, goldminers and early settlers all used them. When they were no longer needed, the horses were let free. Large mobs of wild horses and donkeys now run wild. As they graze, their weight and hard hooves press down the soil. This makes it difficult for some native plants to grow, so there is even less plant food for native animals.

Shipwrecked!

Aboriginal people in Central Australia tell us that cats arrived here long before white people. They say cats came before the donkey, the camel or the rabbit. They say they came in from the west coast, way over Western Australia way, after a shipwreck.

Killer cats

Feral cats are another real pest. They kill and eat our native birds and animals. Smaller marsupials and birds are especially in danger. Like rabbits, cats breed often and their numbers quickly multiply. There are millions of feral cats in Australia.

Across the Desert

Aboriginal people understood the desert country. Thousands of years had taught them how to survive here. It was a very different story for the early European explorers and settlers. They didn't know what to expect. They'd never seen country like it before. Everything was strange to them – the seasons, the plants, the birds and animals. It was incredibly hot and there was often no water. They had a pretty difficult time surviving.

Searching for an inland sea

Early white explorers believed that the middle of Australia must have 'an inland sea' because rivers flowed inland. They felt sure there would be rich country for farm animals and to grow crops. Mostly they found desert.

John McDouall Stuart

John McDouall Stuart was the first white person to cross Australia from south to north. In 1862 he left Adelaide, taking ten men and 71 horses, in yet another attempt to reach the northern coast of Australia. He'd already suffered from heat and thirst, hunger and disease, and been attacked by Aborigines protecting their land.

Ernest Giles

Ernest Giles was another of Australia's inland explorers. Giles covered thousands of kilometres across desert country in the 1870s. He was the first European to record seeing Palm Valley, in the heart of the desert. He also discovered Australia's largest desert, the Great Victoria Desert.

Palm Valley

Stuart's return trip

Stuart's trip to the northern coast and back to Adelaide took more than a year. Although the journey was achieved without any loss of life, Stuart nearly died on the trip back. He was in agony – almost blind and unable to walk. When the group finally arrived back in Adelaide, they were treated like heroes.

John McDouall Stuart

Stuart plants the British flag in the centre of Australia, 1860.

THE OVERLAND TELEGRAPH

When the Overland Telegraph Line opened in 1872, it linked Australia with the rest of the world. It meant we could communicate with other countries in hours, instead of months. That telegraph line was built right across the middle of Australia – across some of the world's harshest desert. The line, more than 3000 km long, closely followed the trail explorer John McDouall Stuart had taken just a few years earlier.

Builders of the Telegraph Line, Roper River, 1872

Building the line

Camels helped carry the food and equipment, including 36 000 poles, and tonnes of wire. Men worked for two years in the dreadful heat. There was little water but plenty of insects. As they went further north, the weather became tropical – hot and steamy.

What's it Called?

Plants, animals, birds and insects all have 'common names' – names we use every day. However, different people sometimes use different names for the same thing. That can be very confusing. So there's also a scientific name, usually in ancient Latin or Greek. That name always stays the same and can be understood anywhere in the world. Here are the common and scientific names of the main plants and animals in this book.

Common Name	Scientific Name
Plants	
bush apple, bush coconut	Cystococcus sp.
bush banana	Marsdenia australis
conkerberry	Carissa lanceolata
desert oak	Allocasuarina decaisneana
desert quandong	Santalum acuminatum
desert yam	Ipomoea costata
hakea, corkwood tree	Hakea spp.
honey grevillea	Grevillea juncifolia
mulga tree	Acacia aneura
native rock fig	Ficus platypoda
parakeelya	Calandrinia balonensis
red cabbage palm	Livistona mariae
spinifex	Triodia spp.
Sturt's desert pea	Clianthus formosus
Sturt's desert rose	Gossypium sturtianum
wild orange	Capparis mitchellii
witchetty bush	Acacia kempeana
Animals	
bearded dragon	Pogona vitticeps
blind snake	Ramphotyphlops sp.

Common Name	Scientific Name
carpet python	Morelia bredli
central netted dragon	Ctenophorus nuchalis
centralian blue tongue lizard	Tiliqua multifasciata
centralian tree frog	Litoria rubella
euro, hill kangaroo	Macropus robustus
frilled lizard	Chlamydosaurus kingii
Gould's sand monitor	Varanus gouldii
knob-tail gecko	Nephrurus laevissimus
mala, rufous hare-wallaby	Lagorchestes hirsutus
perentie	Varanus giganteus
red kangaroo	Macropus rufus
shield shrimp	Triops australiensis
shingleback lizard	Trachydosaurus rugosus
spinifex hopping-mouse	Notomys alexis
spiny-tailed monitor	Varanus acanthurus
thorny devil	Moloch horridus
water-holding frog	Cyclorana maini
Birds	
emu	Dromaius novaehollandiae
galah	Eolophus roseicapilla
spinifex pigeon	Petrophassa plumifera
wedge-tailed eagle	Aquila audax
zebra finch	Poephila guttata
Spiders, Insects, Grubs	
gold-spotted black grasshopper	Monistria sp.
honey ant	Melophorus sp.
lerp scale	Psylla eucalypti
mulga ant	Polyrachis macropus
processionary caterpillar, itchy grub	Ochrogaster contraria
scorpion, rock scorpion	Urodacus sp.
witchetty grub	Cossidae sp.
wolf spider, claypan spider	Lycosa sp.

Glossary

arid — very dry country where rainfall is very low and very unreliable

arid zone — a very dry area (see **arid**)

camouflaged — when the object looks like its surroundings and is hard to see

crustacean — a water animal with a hard shell and antennae, e.g. a yabbie

dormant — sleeping

environment — the earth, the plants and the atmosphere in a particular area

germinate — when a plant develops and grows

gibber — stone or stony desert

gorge — very steep-sided valley

insulation — protection from heat and cold

landform — a feature of the countryside, such as a valley or mountain

larva — an insect at one of the stages before it has grown into its adult shape. Larvae means more than one larva

mammal — an animal that feeds its young on milk

marsupial — an animal that raises its young in a pouch

mesa — a raised area of land with a flat top and steep sides, in a desert

monolith — a huge single block of stone or rock

nocturnal — active at night time

oasis — an area in a desert where there is a natural spring or stream, allowing plants to grow

Outback — inland parts of Australia where very few people live

outcrop — rocky or stony land that rises above the ground

pollinate — carry the pollen from one flower to another for fertilisation

predator — an animal that hunts another animal for food

rainforest — very dense forest supported by very high rainfall

Red Centre — part of Central Australia, especially near the town of Alice Springs. Known for the red colour of the sand and earth

refuge — a place where a plant, animal or person can shelter

semi-arid — dry country that can support grasses and low bushes

species — a type of plant or animal similar to others in a group, but with some differences

tuber — swollen underground stem or bulb of a plant. Some tubers were used as bush food

vegetation — the plants, including grasses and trees, in a certain area

yam — starchy plant, like a sweet potato, used as a bush food

Index

40